JOHN HAY

Masterpieces of

CHINESE ART

NEW YORK GRAPHIC SOCIETY
Greenwich Connecticut

In addition to the Institutions and Collections credited in the notes on the Plates, the Publishers would like to acknowledge the following sources of photographs: Trustees of the British Museum: 33, 37, 41, 45, 48; Fujiyoshi Co., Inc., Tokyo: 15; Robert Harding Associates: 5, 6, 7, 19, 34, 35; Cooper Brothers (Gordon Roberton): 1, 9, 12, 14, 22, 23, 26, 27; Crown Copyright, the Victoria and Albert Museum: 3, 20, 21; Wango H. C. Weng, New York: 30; John Weatherhill, Inc., Tokyo: 39; 19 reproduced from *Treasures and Dynasties of China* by Bamber Gascoigne.

International Standard Book Number 0–8212–0575–7

Library of Congress Catalog Card Number 73–91710

Copyright © 1974 Phaidon Press Ltd

First published in Great Britain 1974 by Phaidon Press Ltd, London

Published in the United States of America and in Canada 1974
by New York Graphic Society Ltd, Greenwich Connecticut 06830
Printed in Great Britain

INTRODUCTION

The art of China has many faces. Some of these, such as celadon porcelain, have been internationally famous for centuries, whilst others, such as the carving of personal seals, are virtually unrecognized in the West. Still others, such as Buddhist sculpture, had long been abandoned in obscurity until rediscovered by connoisseurs, frequently Western, of the present age. The West has played a notable role in this latter process, basically one of breaking down a very rigorous distinction made by the Chinese tradition between art and craftsmanship. Ceramics, as well as sculpture, are an outstanding example of this and it was the West that was largely responsible for bringing it out of the Imperial crockery cupboard onto its podium as one of China's artistic glories. But the West still largely ignores some of the finest expressions of her genius. Calligraphy, for example, which for many people is probably most closely associated with groceries in China Town, in the Chinese tradition is the highest achievement of visual art. Even in painting, a much more obviously universal language, a work can appear with quite different qualities when viewed according to Chinese visual habits.

This book makes no attempt to present an historical survey of China's art; instead it illustrates some of the major themes running consistently through a tradition of many centuries. For the distinctiveness of this tradition is important in the measure to which it further clarifies values that are universal and, in an age when the socio-economic structure that supported China's artistic tradition has finally come asunder, Western artists have begun to explore forms of expression that for centuries were central to that tradition.

The works of art here selected are grouped to represent, firstly, aspects of form (Plates 1–4), material (Plates 5–9) and technique (Plates 10–13). Then follow comparisons of taste in two main spheres of artistic activity, the courtly and the scholarly (Plates 14–25), together with some underlying and enduring trends, especially that of calligraphy (Plates 24–32). The last section (Plates 33–48) illustrates the Chinese artist's approach to a variety of aesthetic choices, such as those between different qualities of line, in dynamics of composition and technique, between linear brushwork and painterly inkwash, and in the balance between representation and expression.

FORM

There is no art without form and the artist's approach to this most basic phenomenon can be endlessly varied. But within a tradition we may sometimes characterize a general approach. The Chinese were certainly particularly conscious of form in its purest presence, unlike the Japanese, for example, whose genius was rather one of texture and pattern. Chinese artists rarely present the visual feasts we find in Japanese art and sometimes perpetrate a dullness, or even a grossness, from which the Japanese were protected by their fine taste. But the Chinese sense of form could achieve expression of such strength and integrity that the rewards of acquaintanceship grow ever greater. The greatest forms of this expression are in ancient bronzes, sculpture, ceramics, and painting and calligraphy.

Plate 1.
BRONZE LIBATION VESSEL, *chüeh* tripod; Shang dynasty, 12th century BC; h. 7½in. British Museum, London.

The *chüeh* is the most distinctive among the many forms of vessel associated with China's Bronze Age. Bronze appeared in China around the sixteenth century BC and so rapidly reached high sophistication of technology and art that some historians suspect the impetus must have been imported from further west. But all the evidence to date indicates that the development took place wholly within China. Its most important phase falls within the Shang period (c. 1600–1027 BC), when the use of metal was confined to a ruling class, which built China's first cities and held a Stone-Age peasantry in thrall. It was not until the 1930s, when the Shang capital city near the modern town of Anyang was excavated, that the twentieth century accepted the Shang and their bronzes as historically authenticated. The bronze vessels are now admired as among the finest of Bronze-Age art.

The Shang rulers formulated elaborate rituals of ancestor worship, some of which entailed hundreds of human sacrifices. The *chüeh* was a wine vessel for ritual libation and various attempts have been made to explain its extraordinary shape in practical terms, such as a derivation from a short horn bound to two bamboo legs. The basic tripod is the most characteristic of early Chinese vessels and the form of the *chüeh*, which still appears tense with ritual purpose even to our modern eyes, shows this essentially practical type shaped by a highly original aesthetic sense. So effectively did this sense serve its ritual master, that when the Shang and their rituals were destroyed by the Chou conquerors, the *chüeh* vanished too.

Plate 2.
GUARDIAN LION, white marble with traces of polychrome; T'ang dynasty, early 8th century; h. 11¾in. Nelson Gallery of Art, Atkins Museum of Fine Arts, Kansas City.

This magnificent lion epitomizes the Chinese genius in sculpture. The art occupies an eccentric position in the Chinese tradition, having flowered in a sudden glory during five centuries of Buddhist influence, from the fourth to the ninth centuries AD, and then rapidly declined into a minor role. In traditional records it is almost wholly the work of anonymous craftsmen and we know nothing of the sculptors of the eighth century, an age when the Chinese sense of form burst forth in an expression of physical vigour unparalleled in China before or since. Although much of it was in the service of Buddhism, this lion is related to an indigenous tradition of guardian figures that can be traced back to the Shang dynasty. By the T'ang dynasty, sacred and secular sculpture had both absorbed the same stylistic influences.

The muscular presence of mid-T'ang sculpture, which was far more physical than that of any other period, certainly reflects influences from north-west India, but these were transformed in an acclamation of the splendour and confidence of the T'ang Empire. In this lion, the bulging muscles, straining tendons, thrusting legs and arching back are all characteristic of sculpture of that age. But it is fascinating to see the strong Chinese tendency towards formal rhythms still at work. The bracing foreleg bulges with muscles that no anatomist would recognize. The head, with its gigantic mouth described by parallel double lines, its broad and protruding eyes, and the curling pattern of its mane, was fashioned by generations of artists rather than by feline genes. The animal itself, of course, is more a creature of mythology than of the jungle and it is the subjection of natural to artistic form that is largely responsible for such monumental power within such a small frame, less than a foot in height.

Plate 3.

STONEWARE JAR, Chün ware;
Chin dynasty, 12th century;
h. 8½in. Victoria and Albert Museum,
London, Eumorfopoulos Collection.

The ceramic wares of the Sung dynasty are perhaps the most highly honoured in the world. Sung potters achieved a directness and a purity of beauty in their shapes and glazes that were an ultimate refinement beyond the greater sophistication of later men. It was a refinement in simplicity and not one of manners.

Sung ceramics were preceded by many centuries of technical development. Indeed, the earliest art of China now known is the decorated Neolithic ware of the fifth millennium BC. Through the thousand years directly preceding the Sung, a continuous process of technical advance can be traced. The wares of the T'ang dynasty gained international fame in their own time and white and green ware was exported in large quantities. Especially fine wares attracted the envy of the court and the finest of the Northern Sung are those that were produced according to Imperial taste in potteries founded for the purpose.

This Chün jar, although of stoneware, is a relative of the blue porcelain produced for the great connoisseur, Emperor Hui-tsung (1101–1126), at the kilns of Ju-chou near the Northern Sung capital of Kai-feng. The kilns of Chün-chou are not far distant and there are many similarities between the two wares, but Chün has a much wider range of quality, only the finest having been made for Imperial use. In this example, made after the Jurchid armies had driven the Chinese court into the south-east, the blue is not so subtle, the body is thicker and the finish less perfect than in the ware of Ju-chou. Nevertheless, it is a magnificent piece, in which the sky-blue freshness of the glaze perfectly complements the expansive fullness of its shape. The simplicity of its form makes many later monochrome wares seem contrived. It has also a tactile quality that comes from the opaqueness of its glaze and Chün is the most fully sensual of all Chinese wares.

Plate 4.

FISHING IN A MOUNTAIN STREAM,
by Hsü Tao-ning;
handscroll with ink on silk (detail);
Northern Sung dynasty, second half of the
11th century;
h. 19in., l. 82in. Nelson Gallery of Art,
Atkins Museum of Fine Arts, Kansas City.

This painting is one of the greatest to survive from the age of monumental landscape art in China, an age that in this sphere is felt by many to be the greatest in the history of the world's art. The painting of landscapes as a subject in their own right is attested by Chinese records of the ninth century. It was a comparatively late development in the history of Chinese painting which, in the sense of individual works by named artists, has its start in the Eastern Chin (317–420). Human subject matter dominated its first six centuries. An art historian of the Northern Sung wrote that the recent overwhelming popularity of landscape painting was one of the most important phenomena in the art of his age. The landscape masters of the late tenth and eleventh centuries achieved such eminence that their styles have been emulated ever since. One of the most important was Li Ch'eng, who was a major influence on Hsü Tao-ning, the painter of this scroll. This influence is seen in motifs such as the bare, clawing tree branches and in the subtly atmospheric reaches of space. It in no way detracts from Hsü Tao-ning's originality: he was, indeed, renowned for his eccentricity and wildly unconventional manner of painting.

The Northern Sung artists were the first to recreate on silk the structure of Nature—not just her individual forms, her vast extent, or her moods, but the absolute integrity of mass and space that can make of landscape an experience profounder than mere visual description, beyond the grasp of intellect. Critics long before the Sung had admired the ability of painters to describe 'a thousand miles within a square inch', but it was not till the Sung that these descriptive abilities were transformed into a power akin to Creation itself. It was this power that led an eleventh-century artist to say that the finest landscape painting was not the one most enjoyable to look at, but the one most worthy of living in. Hsü Tao-ning creates soaring cliffs and sweeping slopes, far-winding valleys and swirling waters, which are as exhilarating as any that Nature could herself provide. The cheerful anglers, more interested in raising a toast across the water than hauling in a fish, invite us to join them with complete conviction.

The miraculous power of art defies the analytic eye, but if we suspend our belief for a moment, we may be amazed at the simplicity of Hsü Tao-ning's formal devices. His motifs, apart from the anglers, are no more than rock, water and trees and there is no startling variation of these. The massive dynamics of his mountains are achieved through elementary rhythms and through tonalities of ink unaided by colour. The depths of his valleys appear through these same tonalities and simply interspaced fingers of shore. The vast expanse of mountain ranges expands out of three simple and distinct spatial sections: a stretch of water in the foreground, a valley between massive cliffs in the middle and a line of disembodied peaks in the far distance. It is this fundamental simplicity which gives Hsü Tao-ning his remarkable power. But it is complemented by a finely judged subtlety of inflection. Thus the curve of each tree branch and the tonality of each brush stroke, every motif and aspect of its execution, all are slightly but constantly varied. The great rhythms are not sapped of strength by over-elaboration, but they sparkle with life. Seldom has an artist so powerfully expressed the forms of his vision.

MATERIAL

In China, the artist's medium was usually subject to firm demarcation. In traditional crafts, of course, this is usually so. Excavations of ancient cities have revealed a clear division between workshops for metal, pottery and bone materials. They each have their own technology and such a division is characteristic of pre-modern societies. But another comparison with Japan shows that the Chinese separation of media has a further dimension. Through the last thousand years, the Japanese developed a milieu in which most aspects of design were intimately associated. A leading painter and a leading textile designer could be one and the same person. This was never so in China, where the medium clearly marked its worker as an artist or a craftsman, a division of profound implications. The most admired painter could never be a designer of textiles, but he might well be prime minister.

Plates 5, 7.

JADE BURIAL SUIT OF THE PRINCESS TOU WAN OF CHUNG-SHAN;
Han dynasty, last decade of the 2nd century BC.
l. 68in.
Chinese Government.

Jade was honoured in China and used for ritual implements as early as Neolithic times. A considerable quantity of Shang dynasty jade carving has survived. By the Han dynasty, the pre-eminence of jade above all minerals was fully established and its various qualities of texture and appearance were said to symbolize the Five Virtues of Charity, Rectitude, Wisdom, Courage and Equity. To it was attributed the power to preserve corpses; hence its use for this burial suit in which 2,156 individual pieces are knotted together mostly with gold thread. The use of gold for this purpose was an Imperial privilege. Chinese jade, a nephrite which is too hard to be sawn by metal, must be cut by abrasive rubbing and this suit may have taken well over a year to complete. Its assembly is also a work of the finest craftsmanship.

The suits of the Princess and her husband, who was buried nearby, are the only complete examples of this practice to have been found. The two tombs were discovered in 1968 and are amongst the most remarkable archaeological discoveries made during China's Cultural Revolution. The prince died in 110 BC, and his wife a few years later.

Plate 6.

TWO LEOPARDS,
parcel-gilt bronze inlaid with garnets and silver;
Han dynasty, late 2nd century BC;
height 4½in. and 4⅝in.
Chinese Government.

These two leopards come from the remarkable treasure found in the tomb of the jade-suited Princess of Chung-shan (see Plates 5, 7) and reflect the superb craftsmanship that served the royal clan, for the Prince of Chung-shan was the emperor's brother. Many of the objects are in metal, which is a clear sign of the standing of the deceased, since metal had become a rare material at this time. Pottery and lacquered wood were commonly substituted.

In the fifth century BC, iron began to supplant bronze in the use of metal for practical implements. At the same time, there was a lively growth in the decorative elaboration of bronze vessels and ornaments. This was made much more splendid by a greatly increased use of parcel-gilt and inlay and the bronze objects inlaid with gold, silver and precious minerals, especially those made during the fourth to the second centuries BC, are amongst the finest of Chinese metalwork. These two leopards show such work at its best, with tensely coiled lines and highly abstracted natural patterns creating a vivid animal spirit. The style owes much in its origins to the Nomad art of the Steppes, brought into China by the warring tribes along her northern marches.

Plate 8.
PORCELAIN STEM CUP, with incised floral design;
Ch'ing dynasty,
mark and period of Ch'ien-lung (1736–95);
diam. 5⅞in.
Percival David Foundation of Chinese Art, London.

Porcelain is one of the most characteristic of all Chinese technological achievements Although China did not develop a tradition of theoretical science, her craftsmen had a genius for pragmatic experimentation which was extraordinarily successful. Porcelain first appears in China around the eighth century AD, nearly a thousand years earlier than in Europe. It is a product of firing, at about 1450° C., a very fine white clay with an addition of powdered feldspar, which thus vitrifies into a glass-like substance. The Chinese defined it by its ability to ring like a bell, whilst in the West its translucency was most admired. Nowadays commonplace, when Europeans first saw Chinese porcelain (and called it 'china'), it was admired as one of man's most remarkable and most mysterious works.

A pure white porcelain was achieved by T'ang dynasty potters and it became the Imperial ware of the early Northern Sung. This stem cup is a work of the eighteenth century, a period when Imperial patronage of ceramic technology reached a peak and the Imperial kilns at Ching-te-chen experimented with almost every major ware of the preceding one thousand years. The cup, with its eggshell-thin body, translucent floral design and clear, ringing tone, is a technical ultimate in porcelain.

Plate 9.
BASKET OF FLOWERS,
woodblock colour print;
Ming dynasty, early 17th century;
h. 11¹³⁄₂₂in., w. 14¼in.
British Museum, London.

Paper was a discovery of the Chinese and is first mentioned in records from the second century AD, when it was rapidly replacing silk and bamboo as a medium for writing. Apart from a bureaucratic importance, its qualities eventually came to play an important role in the arts, especially those of painting and calligraphy. Woodblock printing is also a paper-born art, the notable Chinese achievements in which have not been widely recognized. The early development of woodblock printing was mainly in the cause of religious illustration and the earliest dated woodblock print known is an illustration to a Buddhist scripture, from 868 and now in the British Museum. Two-colour printing appeared in the fourteenth century. By the sixteenth century, five-colour printing for more entertaining purposes, such as erotic manuals, was reaching sophisticated levels in the hands of well-known artists. This charmingly delicate print is purely decorative in purpose, but no lesser in quality than the much better known pattern books for painters, such as the *Treatise for Paintings and Calligraphy of the Ten Bamboo Studio*, of 1633.

TECHNIQUE

The techniques of the artist are, of course, intimately related to his materials. Which aspect is given priority varies according to the context. When the Greeks knew of China as the 'Land of Silk Men' and when Europeans called porcelain 'china', it was the material which was important. But historians would tend to see silk and porcelain in terms of their technologies. Techniques were very important to the Chinese. Indeed, in many ways, such as the running of a glaze or the turning of a brush, the doing often seems more important than the done.

Plate 10.
BRONZE WINE EWER, *kuang*;
Shang period, late 12th century BC;
h. 12⅜in.
The Art Museum, Princeton University.

The ritual vessels of China's Bronze Age are as remarkable for the technology of their manufacture as for their aesthetic impact (see Plates 1, 43). The very complex detail and extremely fine finish shown by much of the decoration was achieved through a most laborious process, that of direct casting from piece-moulds. A model of the desired vessel was first carved in a material such as stone or wood, and then cased in clay. After this case had been baked hard, it was cut into sections and removed with great care, a negative imprint of the vessel on its inner face. The sections were re-assembled around a core shaped to match the hollow interior of the planned vessel and molten bronze was poured in between the core and the assembled piece-mould. After the bronze alloy had hardened, the mould was prised loose, leaving the cast vessel to be filed and smoothed to a perfect finish. The Chinese were unique in applying this foundry method to objects of such amazingly precise complexity as this *kuang*. In fact, it is only within the last two decades that Western experts have come to believe it was possible. The achievement owed much to an exceptional efficiency in furnace design, an efficiency which was already characteristic of China in Neolithic times and which eventually played a major role in the pre-eminence of her ceramic tradition.

Plate 11.
PORCELAIN JAR, with underglaze blue and incised dragons, blue and white ware;
Yüan dynasty, mid-14th century;
h. 20¼in.
Chinese Government.

This superbly decorated vase is one of the most striking examples of Chinese blue and white, which, of all the products of China's artistic tradition, has probably enjoyed the longest and widest fame. Substantial export of this ware to the Middle East began in the fourteenth century and pieces reached Europe soon afterwards. It was tremendously influential on the ceramic industry of both the Middle East and Europe and the results of European attempts to imitate it, beginning in the sixteenth-century faience of Delft and Frankfurt, eventually spawned the well-known pseudo-Chinese willow pattern. In China, the ware went through a continuous evolution up till the eighteenth century, but in all the gigantic output, there are few pieces to match the impact of this fourteenth-century dragon thundering among the waves.

The blue comes from cobalt-oxide pigment and in China the designs were drawn on the raw clay body, which was then coated in a feldspathic glaze and fired as a normal porcelain. The Chinese probably learned the use of this pigment from Persian potters of the late thirteenth century. Their application of it to porcelain became one of the most successful of all their technical achievements.

Lacquering is another technique developed in China, originating in the use of sap from the native lac tree (*rhus verniciflua*) as a paint, which both preserved and decorated wood. The sap, which dries into an extremely hard varnish, was first used as early as the Shang dynasty. By the fourth century BC it was being used with red and black pigment for highly decorative designs on vessels, furniture, musical instruments and a host of other objects. For the following five centuries it was one of the most important materials available to the craftsman.

During later centuries, lacquer was supplanted in many of its uses by ceramic and other materials but, by the fourteenth century, the decorative arts had developed a very specialized technique of carved lacquer. In this, up to two hundred layers were painted onto a core of wood reinforced with fabric, building up a thickness of several milli-metres. After this process, which could last for several years, the lacquer was sufficiently deep and hard for elaborate carving.

These two boxes come from the phase of carved lacquer that is most highly regarded for its colour and its balance between artistry and virtuosity. A number of other materials, such as bamboo, jade and rhinoceros horn, were also used commonly by centuries of supremely skilled Chinese carvers. Their subjects were often drawn from an ancient pictorial tradition, rather than a purely ornamental vocabulary. In their finest work, such as the narcissus on the larger of these two boxes, the motifs seem to float free of their ground. The smaller box is an early example of a characteristic Chinese style, used for carving scenes of figures in architectural and garden settings. In it, a variety of ingeni-ously stylized diaper designs represent ground and water, at the same time providing a decorative background for three-dimensional motifs.

In the Chinese tradition, the border between craft and fine art passes through the fields of painting, dividing 'professionals' from 'amateurs'. Professional painters served the masters of imitation and decoration, their work was condemned to superficiality by a technical concern for similitude. The amateurs were inheritors of the humanist tradition, either serving in the civil service or simply cultivating the life of an educated gentleman. Painting, for them, was the aesthetic exercise of the moral, intellectual and spiritual faculties. Since China's history was recorded by her educated elite, it is this elitist history of painting that we have received. Both as history and theory it may make strange sense, but, as a creative force applied to the 'amateur' art of the *literati* themselves, its results were positive and profound.

The painter in the amateur tradition was at once more scornful of technical expertise and more strictly ordered by it than painters of any other tradition. The root of this fact was in his brush, essentially the same as was used in calligraphy (see Plate 30) and which, in the practice of writing, he would wield daily from the age when his education first began. Some pictorial subjects were exceptionally well suited to the scholar's brush and ink. A leaf of bamboo, for instance, may emerge from a flick of the writing brush—although it will need years of practice before it will have the crisp strength of an actual leaf, before it will seem to twist and curl in the air. The painter seeks the life of the bamboo, not its form.

The subjects of this work by Chang Yen-fu had started to become popular around the late eleventh century, when the ideals of amateur painting were being formulated. Chang's superbly sensitive rendering—a highly sophisticated souvenir of an elegant literary party—is surrounded by admiring comments and poems written by friends and signed with their seals. The seals of later collectors decorate the borders.

Plate 12.
LACQUER BOXES,
Ming dynasty, early 15th century;
diam. of the larger 5⅛in.; of the smaller 3⅜in.
British Museum, London.

Plate 13.
BAMBOO, THORNS AND A PAIR OF BIRDS,
by Chang Yen-fu;
hanging scroll with ink on paper;
Yüan dynasty, second quarter of the 14th century;
h. 30 in.
Nelson Gallery of Art, Atkins Museum of Fine Arts, Kansas City.

IMPERIAL AND SCHOLARLY TASTE

It would be misleading to make a rigid division between scholarly taste and Imperial taste at the court, which, from the Sung dynasty onwards, was increasingly regarded as fostering craft, rather than art. But the two spheres did favour different aesthetic forms, a situation intensified by the great resources of labour and technology at the emperors' command. A comparison reveals both consistency and variety and the following three pairs of objects illustrate moments of Imperial taste from the Ming, Sung and T'ang dynasties.

A late-Ming connoisseur, writing of Ming enamelled ware, commented: 'The finest wares of the Ch'eng-hua reign are unsurpassed. The stemmed cups with everted rims and round, shallow bodies, painted with grapes in enamels of five colours, are incomparably finer than those of the earlier Hsüan-te reign. Next in quality are the toasting cups, decorated with plants and insects, or a hen and chickens . . .' Another man wrote that the luxury-loving Emperor Wan-li (1570–1620) always had a pair of Ch'eng-hua chicken cups on his dining table, which, even then, were worth 100,000 cash. In Ming ceramics, it is the use of coloured enamels that seems to have best expressed Imperial tastes. The Chinese call this ware *tou-ts'ai*, literally 'colours competing for effect', and in its development following the Ch'eng-hua reign this 'competition' becomes increasingly strident.

Lü Chi was a painter at court, whose career embraced the Ch'eng-hua reign (1465–87) and whose work represents court taste of the time as well as do the five-colour enamelled cups. This painting is one of a set of 'the four seasons', a favourite subject for screen paintings, and mounted as a screen it would certainly appear superbly effective in a lavish palace hall. It is painted with a brush basically similar to that used by Chang Yen-fu, although somewhat larger and firmer (Plate 13). The interest here, however, is in the virtuoso conjuring of powerful rhythms in a dramatically decorative design. Silk is better suited than paper to this purpose.

The celadon-green porcelain of the twelfth century has a rich and almost luscious glaze that is miraculously balanced by a cool, translucent purity. Later celadon tends to lose this balance in favour of the former qualities. The green of these wares, resulting from ferrous oxides in the glaze, is a colour that Chinese potters began to develop in the Han period. The results of this development eventually became closely associated with Imperial wares of the Southern Sung. Of all glazes, perhaps celadon appealed most to Chinese poets, one of whom wrote that, 'The kilns of Yüeh bring forth the moist September weather, stealing brilliant greens from a thousand mountains.'

The Southern Sung is often described as a supremely elegant age, fostered by an increasingly introverted court. The first emperor re-established the royal academy of fine arts which had become famous under the Emperor Hui-tsung in the northern capital (see Plate 28). Later, the painter Ma Yüan became one of the most famous to serve in this institution. His fastidious fingers here select from nature's most exquisite moods a line of visual poetry and his cool elegance perfectly complements the celadon porcelain of the same age. The delicate asymmetry of the composition, contained within an intimate format, is typical of the court academy style. In its space is suspended a poem, written by the gracious hand of an empress:

They greet the wind with artful charm,
Boasting pink beauty moist with dew.

The court of the T'ang dynasty at its apogee was the most glorious in China's history, honoured as at no other time by a galaxy of intellectual and artistic talent. The theme of this painting comes from a disaster that shattered it in 756, when a rebellious general forced the emperor into temporary exile. Although the throne was restored, the court's prestige inevitably declined. The original drama and distress of the emperor's flight is transformed by this picture into a stately picnic.

The T'ang was a great era of mural painting, which was then practised by all the greatest painters. This was never again the case. Mural art had to make a dramatic impact, in terms of both narrative clarity and architectural embellishment. This painting, although later in execution, may be seen as a reduced version of a once great mural. The fine contour drawing and the rich, decorative colouring are a classic manner of the T'ang.

Metalwork of the T'ang dynasty is one of the finest expressions of T'ang craftsmanship. It is also a particularly vivid witness to the international prestige and cosmopolitan nature of the empire, for many of its forms and decorative motifs were ultimately derived from Iranian art. A great deal of trade was carried on by the overland Silk Road, which ran through the Central Asian desert towns and far on to the Middle East, where there was a great tradition of craftsmanship in metalwork. Traders brought many examples of it to China and craftsmen came too. The lotus petals forming the sides of this bowl are an ancient Chinese adaptation of a motif from Buddhist art. The prancing animals come from an indigenous tradition, whilst the background of flowers and dots shows strong

Iranian influence. Vessels of gold and silver were periodically restricted by law to use by the aristocracy and the Imperial palaces must have held great quantities. This bowl comes from an extraordinary hoard found within the bounds of the T'ang capital, on the site of a mansion of the Prince of Pin. Over a thousand pieces of gold, silver and mineral treasure had been buried in earthenware pots, probably in the year 756, when the city was overrun by rebel troops (see Plate 18).

Silk was one of the most enduring accompaniments to the good life in China. The silkworm was cultivated as early as Neolithic times and silk became the first commodity for which the country was internationally renowned. Rome knew of China as the source of the diaphanous fabrics scandalously flaunted by her high society. Recent archaeological discoveries have revealed a very wide range of luxury silk fabrics made in the Han dynasty.

The most important later development in Chinese textiles was the *k'o-ssu* ('cut-silk') tapestry, an extremely laborious technique which was introduced into China from Western Asia and perfected around the eleventh century. This Chinese fabric, which was unmatched in the fineness of its weave, was in its turn introduced to medieval Europe, where it greatly influenced the textile industry. In China, the development of *k'o-ssu* tapestry was closely related to garments of the aristocracy, the patterns of which were often strictly regulated. The most famous examples of this are the *lung-p'ao* ('dragon robes') worn by the emperors. This late but splendid specimen bears the five-clawed Imperial dragon.

Plate 20.
IMPERIAL DRAGON ROBE,
k'o-ssu tapestry (detail of chest panel);
Ch'ing, late 18th century.
Victoria and Albert Museum, London,
Vuilleymier Collection.

THE POTTER OUTSIDE THE IMPERIAL KILNS

The Sung dynasty saw the development of many important and beautiful ceramic wares at various removes from the Imperially patronized monochrome porcelains. Most are stoneware, made with coarser paste and baked at a slightly lower temperature than was porcelain. Their full range is only nowadays becoming apparent, but the three well known categories of Chün, Chien and Tz'u-chou represent a considerable variety.

Plate 21.
STONEWARE VASE,
Tz'u-chou ware;
Sung dynasty, probably 12th century;
h. 9½in.
Victoria and Albert Museum, London.

This most handsome vase represents a ware which, in recent times, has found its most enthusiastic admirers outside of China. It is called Tz'u-chou ware after a kiln site in Hopei province, in the north of China, but in fact it was widely manufactured as a popular ware for the humbler ranks of society. It is usually decorated with vigorous designs which, as in this spray of peony, are often painted in brown in a thin clay paste known as slip, or else scraped out of a slip with which the vessel is first covered. Both techniques, far more than was the case with the carving and moulding of aristocratic monochrome porcelains, encouraged a delightful liveliness. This quality also shows how influential were the patterns of the traditional Chinese brush, even in ornament. But of all Sung wares, the plebeian Tz'u-chou has the most realistic motifs. This trend was taken up by Imperial wares of the Ming dynasty, although rarely with such strength.

Plate 22.
STONEWARE DISH,
Chün ware;
Chin dynasty, 13th century;
diam. 7¼in.
Percival David Foundation of Art, London.

Pale blue Chün ware has already been illustrated by the jar in Plate 3. This stoneware dish bears the purple splashes which developed as the most distinctive feature of the ware. Such examples produced from the eleventh to the twelfth centuries have attracted the particular admiration of Western connoisseurs. The purple probably results from traces of copper in the feldspathic glaze and, like the splashed three-coloured glazes of the T'ang dynasty, may have developed through the exploitation of an initially accidental effect. The potters for a time managed to retain a sense of such accident, which gives their design an elusiveness fascinating to our modern eyes. Much of Chün ware was made for common use, a situation which would have fostered artistic licence rather than technical perfection.

Plate 23.
STONEWARE VASE, northern black ware;
Sung dynasty, probably early 12th century;
h. 10{7/10}in.
British Museum, London.

In south-east China a ware called Chien, after the area of manufacture, began to appear in the tenth century. Its brown to black, iron-pigmented glaze is often streaked and spotted in a characteristic fur-like appearance. The floral design on this example is associated with a later phase, when similar wares were made in a number of kilns, both north and south. The vase, with its gracefully swelling body and fugitive beauty in the dancing rhythms of its decoration, is very fine. It shares with much of Chün ware a perfectly judged effect of casualness and seems much more sophisticated than the wares associated with Tz'u-chou (Plate 21). Chien ware originally developed as vessels for drinking tea and in this connection became very influential in Japan. Its beauty, one of subtlety rather than of perfection, may represent the highly cultivated aestheticism of a scholarly class.

Plate 24.

A MYRIAD PETALS OF JADE,
by Ch'en Hsien-chang;
hanging scroll with ink on silk;
dated 1437, Ming dynasty;
h. 44in., w. 22⅝in.
National Palace Museum, Taiwan.

The plum tree, blossoming in winter, was a much loved theme for the Chinese poet and painter. This rustic and ancient branch of cascading blossom, painted in the cool purity of ink alone, has a beauty that differs utterly from the exquisite vignette of an apricot sprig in the palace garden (Plate 17). A poem that was written by another great painter of plum blossom, Wang Mien (d. 1366), says much to explain this:

> The north wind, blowing cold, strips the luxuriant trees;
> Wet rocks roll rumbling through barren valleys.
> Homesteads deep in the wilds see few men pass;
> The cold plum alone stands against the cold blue.
> It is jade, shining brightly, unbesmirched;
> Before the spring wind comes, the blossoms open themselves.
> A life of purity and humility will be its own guard . . .
> The plum blossoms and I sing the same tune. . . .

Plate 25.

PAVILION OF THE LUXURIANT TREES,
by Shen Shih-ch'ung;
album leaf with ink and colour on paper,
second in an album of 12 leaves depicting
gardens, probably in the suburbs of Sung-
chiang;
dated 1625, Ming dynasty;
h. 11⅞in., w. 18¾in.
National Palace Museum, Taiwan.

The ancient cities of south-east China, the most sophisticated cultural centre in post-Han times, were much loved for their many famous gardens. The Chinese garden, which reached a philosophical eminence during the Ming dynasty, was a concept of great subtlety and intricacy, attempting to create within its walls the multiplicity and variability of nature's own forms. Mountains and rivers were made in miniature, laid out in a dense complex of scenarios, each of which could be contemplated in its perfection from a carefully located pavilion. Such pavilions were ideal for the elegant pursuits of scholars, writers and artists and many Chinese paintings are inscribed as 'painted in such-and-such a pavilion'. This picture by Shen Shih-ch'ung is a garden scene of particular enchantment, with a gracious sweep of shimmering pines sliding softly into mists which marvellously evokes the pavilion's name. It comes from a set painted for Wang Shih-min, a native of Sung-chiang and one of the most honoured scholars and artists of that time.

THE DISCIPLINE OF PAINTING

There is a great contrast in aesthetic tone between the celadon jar (Plate 16) and the Chien vase (Plate 23). The contrast seems similar to that between Ma Yüan's sprig of apricot (Plate 17) and Ch'en Hsien-chang's hoary plum branch (Plate 24). Whilst it is difficult to describe much of a sociological dimension in the contrast between ceramics, it is much easier to do so in the case of the paintings. One clearly speaks with the refined manners of the court; the other, in both subject and technique, symbolizes succinctly the moral discipline of the idealistic Confucian scholar. The scholars, whether employed in their traditional function as bureaucratic backbone of the state, or cultivating themselves in retirement, evolved an elaborate aesthetic language. They tended towards expressions of subtlety and restraint, sometimes of an extraordinary dullness, but sometimes achieving a profound beauty and strength. Many of their artistic concerns were naturally shared by other groups of artists, but the network of these concerns, where they mesh within the *literatus* experience, has an unmistakable character.

Plates 26, 27.

PAINTING AND POEM,
by Tao-chi (1640–c. 1717);
album leaves with ink and colour on paper,
from an album of 12 paintings;
Ch'ing dynasty;
h. of painting 11in.
Collection of Madame Ling Su-hua,
London.

For an artist working within a circle of close friends, the most congenial format was the album, rather than the vertical hanging scroll or the horizontal table scroll. In the seventeenth century, when many painters became very introspective within such groups, this most withdrawn of formats was put to many fascinating uses. An album is executed and seen as a book, to be placed on the table and savoured with leisurely intimacy, page by page. Usually, a painting is mounted on the right and faced on the left by calligraphy. The latter may be poems, accounts of a social occasion or personal comments, which may be written at the same time as the painting or after it has been mounted, and it may be by the painter himself, his companions, or any other subsequent admirer. An album can be a composite work of extraordinary complexity. Tao-chi was one of the greatest and most original artists of the seventeenth century. In this album, both painting and calligraphy are from his hand, works of equal art, forming intimate images of a very personal landscape. The manner of both painting and calligraphy varies greatly from leaf to leaf, but they all belong together as a coherent whole.

The painter himself, in this leaf, gazes out of a wicker window. Only the sounds of a waterfall echo his thoughts, while a solitary pine curls companionably over his roof. The composition has a fascinating division, between the intimacy of the pavilion in its lower half and above, separated by a river, rocky cliffs topped with mist-drenched pines. Tao-chi's poem reads:

> The traces of the ages here are scarce touched by man;
> A world that is half of the mountains, half of the waters.
> A small pavilion against the stream, where the heat of summer quickly ebbs,
> And the cool of mists under a bright sky seeps through my clothes.
> Painted in the Pavilion of the Pine of our Country's Longevity, at the Eastern Villa.

THE FIVE-COLOURED PARAKEET,
painting and calligraphy by the Emperor
Hui-tsung (1101–25);
horizontal scroll with ink and colour on
silk (two details);
Northern Sung dynasty;
h. 20⅞in.
Museum of Fine Arts, Boston, Maria
Antoinette Evans Fund.

The practice of adjoining painting and writing goes back in China to the earliest forms of pictorial art. Its purpose was originally textual elucidation and it was facilitated by both word and picture being executed on the same ground with the same instruments. As early as the T'ang dynasty it was said that painting and calligraphy were 'one way', but this concept went through varying interpretations over the centuries.

In this work, the inscription beside the painting has clearly been raised to the same aesthetic status. The Emperor Hui-tsung, whose reign collapsed in military humiliation, excelled as a painter of birds and flowers and was famous for his personal style of calligraphy, known as 'slender gold wire'. There is a surgical precision of brush stroke, and the manneristic extremes of stroke-formation and balance, executed with knife-point clarity, are characteristics of the calligraphy which can also be traced in the painting.

CALLIGRAPHY

Calligraphy, in the estimation of the Chinese, is the greatest visual art. Its unique characteristics, as an abstract art with a conventionally understood vocabulary of forms, bestowed an extraordinary stability which, hopefully, may contribute to its eventual recognition as China's greatest contribution to the aesthetic consciousness of the world.

Of all arts, calligraphy offers the most direct expression, in enduring form, of the artist's vision. It is executed with a finely pointed brush, the resilient head of which is usually made from the hairs of a sable-like animal, or a goat. The brush is so important that the making of its many varieties is a highly specialized art. In writing, it is controlled with extreme precision, achieved by exhaustive training of every muscle and faculty involved. The finest writer must be able to direct, turn, twist, raise and lower the point through the minutest inflections and with complete muscular fluency. The shape of the brush and the lie of its hairs must be totally at his command. Of nearly equal importance is the consistency of the ink—carefully blended for the moment from water and a preparation of pine soot—the loading of the ink in the brush and its flow onto the paper. There is no more sensitive instrument for the recording of every psychological and muscular pulse of the artist. Transmitted from his body, through his shoulder, arm, hand and fingers, the entirety of his aesthetic consciousness flows out in an acutely physical experience and takes form in the line, the structure and balance of each character and the shape of the whole passage. A piece of calligraphy may be no more than a passage of information, or it may use a text simply as a vehicle for calligraphic form, or it may fuse content and form in equal worth.

Plate 30.

A POEM OF FAREWELL TO A FRIEND,
calligraphy in formal script,
by Yeh-lü Ch'u-ts'ai;
handscroll with ink on paper (detail);
dated 1240, pre-Imperial Yüan;
h. 14⅜in., l. 111⅛in.
Collection of John M. Crawford, Jr., New
York.

Yeh-lü Ch'u-ts'ai, a character of nobility and rugged strength, was a Khitan aristocrat who served Genghis Khan as prime minister when the Mongols were extending their control over north China. He was deeply cultivated in the Chinese tradition and probably did more than any other man to soften the harshness of the Mongols' conquest. He wrote this poem in farewell to an admired friend: 'Half the common folk have fled the dangerous north-western regions; only those under your administration have felt surrounded by security. . . .'

The blunt strength of Yeh-lü Ch'u-ts'ai's calligraphy makes an extreme contrast with the mannered elegance of the Emperor Hui-tsung (Plate 29). In viewing calligraphy, the crucial experience is a temporal process of reading the original course of the artist's brush through its traces in ink. The sequence and direction of strokes within a character are given by convention, with this knowledge and a working experience of calligraphy, any educated Chinese could visualize the motion of the brush from start to finish. Its dynamic qualities are peculiar to every artist. Sometimes, as in the rapid and abbreviated manner of Chu Yün-ming (Plate 31), movement itself becomes a dominating drive. The Emperor Hui-tsung writes a much more formal script, but his individual strokes have dash and brilliance. With Yeh-lü Ch'u-ts'ai, the sequence and direction of the strokes is still crucial, but we admire the grave and weighty articulation of massive strength. This writing, with its punishing integrity of purpose, is one of the finest pieces of calligraphy extant.

Plate 31.

POEMS ON FLOWERS,
calligraphy in draft-script by Chu Yün-ming
(1460–1526);
handscroll with ink on paper (detail);
dated 1519, Ming dynasty;
h. 18in., l. 624¾in.
The Art Museum, Princeton University,
Anonymous loan.

The calligraphy of Chu Yün-ming releases movement to dominate the entire form. The Chinese have always liked to say that in calligraphy a man's nature cannot be concealed and this is most obviously true with those artists who favoured the draft-script. This script developed at the end of the Han period as a short-hand, but eventually became the most purely aesthetic form. Chu Yün-ming was the greatest genius of this art during the Ming dynasty and was also famed for his riotous delight in gay living. His calligraphy epitomizes a belief, developed over the centuries, that the ultimate aim of technical practice is to break free from all technical effort. As with great sportsmen, his skill is so effortless that it seems invisible but, were the innate skill to falter, the illusion at once would stumble. The canons of the art still apply with a strictness unrelaxed.

In calligraphy, the artist's performance materializes at the tip of his brush into a form existing in both space and time. Even in perpetual stillness, movement can still be its essence. In this process Chu Yün-ming explores a phenomenon which has fascinated many modern artists: accident in art. Within the effortless rule of his experience, he exults in the excitement of form spilling out in the ink from his brush. He controls the brush with absolute precision but the form is an accident of its passage through the moment and can never be fully repeated by conscious intent.

AESTHETIC CHOICES

The remaining works in this selection illustrate qualities resulting from the artist's choice between a variety of aesthetic poles, such as the linearity of the brush and the painterliness of the ink, between the rhythm of execution and the stability of structure, between descriptive representation and expressive distortion. Many of these qualities could be illustrated in calligraphy, but whilst some of them undoubtedly were formulated through calligraphy, others seem to have stemmed from fundamental habits of visualization with extraordinary tenacity and vigour. Since the purpose of this book is, in part, to show how these qualities may be seen in a wide range of Chinese art, the selection has been made to reflect this variety.

Plate 32.

TARTARS TRAVELLING ON HORSEBACK,
by Li Tsan-hua (899–937);
handscroll with ink and colours on silk
(detail); 10th century, Later T'ang.
Museum of Fine Arts, Boston, Keith
McLeod Fund.

Plate 33.

VAGRANTS, by Wu Wei;
handscroll with ink and slight colour on
paper (detail);
Ming dynasty;
h. 14¾in., l. 201 7⁄16in.
British Museum, London.

Plate 34.

THE FLYING HORSE,
bronze tomb figure;
Later Han dynasty, mid-2nd century AD;
from Wu-wei, Kansu province;
h. 9⅝in.
Chinese Government.

Plate 35.

TOMB GUARDIAN,
pottery figurine with three coloured glazes;
T'ang dynasty, first half of the 8th century;
excavated from a tomb at Ch'ung-p'u, near
Sian, Shensi province, in 1959;
h. 25 25⁄32in.
Chinese Government.

The linear quality of Chinese art has often been noted. In painting, it is easy to attribute it to the relationship with calligraphy, but, in fact, the nature of this relationship varies tremendously. These horses, the work of a Khitan Tartar prince who lived as a Chinese subject and devoted himself to the tradition of Chinese painting, are drawn with the 'iron-wire line' which was a technical tradition at least as old as the Eastern Chin (317–420). The thin line is allowed only the finest variation and it discovers the contours of form with the precision of a scalpel. In calligraphy, line is form with its own contours; here it is but the contour of another form.

This vagrant uproar finds China's lofty aesthetic tradition making ribald fun of itself, and doing so with superb artistry. The previous illustration is of an eminently respectable subject portrayed in a most refined manner, but this scene is utterly beneath the dignity of a Confucian scholar and is painted with apparent coarseness. The Chinese artist often expresses the quality of his subject in the quality of a line.

Wu Wei, an artist of eccentric mirth, found himself uncongenially employed at court and was brash enough to leave. He signs this painting with his eminent rank, which makes it seem a deliberately vulgar gesture. But there is nothing vulgar about his skill, in which the influence of calligraphy is clearly visible. A comparison with the writing of Chu Yün-ming (Plate 31) will show this. Both calligrapher and painter have the same fluent control of the play of the brush hairs and the flow of the ink. Form is within the line itself.

This horse, since its recovery from a general's grave, in 1969, has achieved greater international fame than any other work of Chinese art. It was one of several dozen bronze statuettes, each of the highest quality, found in the tomb and presumably made as funerary ware. The horse was a creature of great practical and symbolic importance to the Chinese; vital for bearing their arms against the warriors who pressed on the northern frontier and an embodiment of nobility, swiftness, strength and endurance.

Art of the Han dynasty is remarkable for its rhythmic vitality, delighting in dancing line that curves with energy pent. Often its forms are quite abstract, but in this horse it finds a perfect harmony with representation, although, anatomically speaking, the beast is not so convincingly integrated as the famous horses of the T'ang dynasty are. A fleeting touch with earth is marvellously suggested by the flying swallow under one hoof. The swift genius of Han art was absorbed into an ever widening spectrum of artistry, but it was never wholly lost. The flying swallow was the metaphor for a swift horse, as in the description of such a creature by a fifth-century poet: 'The flying swallow soars over wide-flung roads, the fish-hawk sports by the pure shores'.

The fiery figures, who have been so frequently found protecting tombs of the T'ang dynasty, are a distinctive amalgam of Chinese and Buddhist mythology. Their anger was to frighten off harmful influences and the expression of this gave T'ang sculptors a splendid chance to indulge a Chinese passion for formal rhythms. Although there is still an affinity with the liveliness of Han art, long inherent qualities have been given a new weight by the powerful plasticity of T'ang sculpture. The vigorous rhythms of these tomb figures become even more vibrant through the green, yellow and brown glazes, freely applied and even more freely spread by the firing.

Plate 36.
BUDDHA WITH TWO BODHISATTVAS AND TWO
DISCIPLES,
gilt-bronze shrine;
Northern Wei dynasty, first quarter of the
6th century;
h. 23¼in.
Metropolitan Museum, New York.

Plate 37.
'ON THE BANK IS A MAGPIE'S NEST',
from the illustrations of the 'Odes of
Ch'en', by Ma Ho-chih;
handscroll with ink and colour on silk
(detail of seventh section);
Southern Sung dynasty, 12th century;
h. 10 9/16in., l. 287¾in.
British Museum, London.

Plate 38.
THE NORTHERN SEA,
by Chou Ch'en;
handscroll with ink and slight colour on
silk (detail);
Ming dynasty, early 16th century;
h. 11 8/16in., l. 53¼in.
Nelson Gallery of Art, Atkins Museum of
Fine Arts, Kansas City.

Plate 39.
BRIGHT MISTS IN A MOUNTAIN VILLAGE,
by Yü-chien;
originally from a set of Eight Views of
the Hsiao and Hsiang Rivers;
handscroll with ink on paper (detail);
Southern Sung dynasty, 13th century;
h. 13in.
Collection of Ayako Yoshikawa, Tokyo.

Plate 40.
THE COMING OF AUTUMN, by Hung-jen;
hanging scroll with ink on paper;
Ch'ing dynasty, mid-17th century;
h. 48½in., w. 24¾in.
Honolulu Academy of Arts, Honolulu,
Wilhemina Tenney Memorial Collection.

The Chinese predilection for the expression of form through linear rhythm is seen to superb advantage in China's adaptation of Indian and Central Asian sculptural styles, which followed the introduction of Buddhism and its art. Although the transformation was most dramatically pursued in the great cave temples, some of the smaller, portable cult figures of bronze, especially those of the sixth century, are among the greatest of the world's religious works of art. In this example, with the Buddha bestowing protection, at the still centre of the composition rests the face, its sharply-cut features those of a spirit that is in the absolute calm of perfect knowledge. From this face, the composition opens downwards to embrace the worshipper and then flames exultantly upwards, through the trailing robes of the attending *apsaras* who float around the mandorla screen. No religious work could offer the believer a more gloriously transcendental experience.

Some Chinese painters developed manners in which the line itself has such a personal quality as to be instantly recognizable. Ma Ho-chih is one of the greatest of such artists. At the command of his emperor, he painted a very extensive series of scrolls to illustrate classical texts which, in the Chinese context, may fairly be described as scriptures of the state. The *Book of Odes*, supposedly edited by Confucius and amongst the earliest of surviving Chinese texts, is a heterogeneous collection of poetry, which Confucian scholars succeeded in re-interpreting as political allegory. The poem illustrated here plainly was once a lover's lament on a partner deceived by jealous lies. It begins:

> On the bank is a magpie's nest,
> On the hill grows vetch—
> Who has misled my sweetheart?
> Oh! How my heart fills with grief.

Beside each of Ma Ho-chih's illustrations of these poems, the emperor himself wrote the text.

Ma Ho-chih could not have developed his distinctive manner without the concept of calligraphic control applied to brushwork in painting, a concept which was formulated in the eleventh century. But he is supreme in his ability to endow each stroke with the same vibrant life, so that every motif, be it tree, rock, water, human or any other, sings in unison. We may be reminded of Wei dynasty sculpture (Plate 36), but the extroverted anonymity of the worshipper is here replaced by the inward vision of an artist.

The Chinese term for a landscape is 'mountain and water'. These two elements are its bones. Trees and similar motifs are secondary features, like hair on a head. When the subject is taken as a philosophical category, there is a tendency to keep a rational balance between the main elements. But an artist interested in more visual matter might concentrate on a more specific aspect. This picture is a superb example of such an approach. Although the Northern Sea is a mythological, rather than a geographical subject, Chou Ch'en conjures up a very tangible storm in a dynamic image of waves and trees. At the end of the scroll, on the left, a cliff rears up in defiance. The sinuous lines of tree trunks and the massed detail of foilage are an obvious pleasure for the painter's brush, but in the elusive currents of water there is pure joy. Chou Ch'en was closely associated with contemporary scholars, but was himself an artist of thoroughly professional standards, as is shown by the clarity with which he works out the dense rhythms of this composition.

This is the work of one of a group of Zen priest-painters, who sometimes attempted to throw off all strictures of technical convention. There is no obvious sign here of calligraphic discipline or respect for the form of the traditional brush. The Northern Sea by Chou Ch'en (Plate 38) depicts a scene of natural violence with brushwork that is itself unmoved by the experience. This work by Yü-chien depicts a scene of softness and quietness with a violent technique. The underlying approach to technique still owes most to calligraphy. But Yü-chien has almost completely turned brush values into ink values, finding an original solution to the dichotomy between these two. The dichotomy underlies many of the choices open to Chinese calligraphers and painters and, in the vivid vocabulary of their criticism, is often discussed as the relationship between 'bone' and 'flesh'.

The patterns and rhythms arising in massed brush strokes often inveigled Chinese painters into compositions of extraordinary complexity. On the other hand, the simplicity of line and the purity of paper attracted artists of stillness and ascetic restraint. The most famous of such artists was Ni Tsan, a fourteenth-century master whose obsession with cleanliness was matched by the sparseness of his landscapes. Hung-jen, one of the famous individualists of the seventeenth century, plainly admired Ni Tsan and explored his manner with extreme sensitivity. He reduces landscape to the barest minimum capable of sustaining its structure. It is practically all brush and has hardly any inkwash. Such stillness would become deadness, were it not for the subtleties of dynamics and texture in the line itself. Hung-jen here uses this manner to evoke the clarity of Autumn, when frost and wind have swept the landscape clean of Summer's lushness. It was this aspect of Autumn, rather than the riot of turning colour, which most appealed to the Chinese.

Plate 41.
BODHISATTVA,
sandstone statue;
Northern Ch'i dynasty, 6th century;
h. 65¾in.
British Museum, London.

A Bodhisattva is the highest stage of being below that of Buddhahood. In Buddhist art, the range of artistic problems encompassed by Chinese sculptors during the sixth to the eighth centuries is both impressive and fascinating. In the sculpture of Northern Wei (Plate 36) we see mass itself completely translated into linear rhythm. In the greatness of T'ang (Plates 2, 35), mass and form are fused in a powerful statement of weight. Northern Ch'i sculpture is one of the stages intermediate between these two. The volume of the figure is reduced, with extraordinary rigour, to a massively smooth column. The accoutrements, in this case drawn from a tradition of princely attire, are hung on this mass in a screen of great delicacy and elegance. Such a disciplined and almost philosophical reduction of the physical world into two opposite poles of structure and ornamentation is constantly found in Chinese thought and art. In landscape painting it is expressed in terms of mountains and their surface features, such as trees. There is something of this philosophy in Hung-jen's The Coming of Autumn (Plate 40).

DISTORTION

The function of distortion in Chinese art is a question of great interest. As in the West, it is a potent expressionistic device. But this is often obscured by the fact that, to many Western eyes, the whole of Chinese art is characterized by distortion. Any art can represent acceptably the physical world only by courtesy of certain visual conventions, and eyes trained within the conventions of one culture will always tend to interpret those of another culture as heretical 'distortions'. An outstanding case is the highly selective conventions of three-dimensional representation to which the West has become so accustomed that they seem to many people an inherent desideratum of pictorial art. They are, of course, no such thing. Other conventions for comprehending form, such as modulation of a contour line, are neither less nor more inherently justified. When the crucial conventions of Chinese art are known, it becomes possible to judge what can properly be called distortion in this context.

Plate 42.
IMMORTALITY UNDER THE GREAT PINE,
by Ch'en Hung-shou;
hanging scroll with ink and bright colours on silk;
dated 1635, Ming dynasty;
h. 79½in., w. 38½in.
National Palace Museum, Taiwan.

Ch'en Hung-shou, an artist whose reputation is only now rising to deserved heights, is one of the most fascinating of all Chinese painters in his use of distortion. Although his manner seems so eccentric, he reached it largely through an extensive study of ancient masters. This must have helped him realize how, in fact, art does pass historically through fundamental changes in modes of visualization. His paintings appear as comments on the fact that an ancient work, through its very strangeness, can jolt the eye into transmitting an image with extraordinary impact.

This painting, on which the artist himself has written a poem in archaic metre, speaks with just such an unforgettable voice. The old scholar's face is one of the most powerful in Chinese art. Ch'en Hung-shou lived in the late Ming dynasty, when a sudden disintegration of the cultural nexus led to a fantastic explosion of very personal artistic manners. He and others used vehicles such as distortion to carry a weight of overt expressionism that was rarely matched before or after.

Plate 43.
BRONZE WINE CONTAINER, *yu*;
Shang dynasty, c. 12th century BC;
h. 7in.
Honolulu Academy of Arts, Honolulu, Wilhemina Tenney Memorial Collection.

A quest for expressive power and distortion in Chinese art must inevitably turn back to bronze décor of the Shang dynasty. It surely belonged to an age when art still served the ritual of magic and its forms were essentially vessels for a supernatural power. But such art is often careless of visual and technical precision and the extraordinary refinement of the Shang craftsmen probably indicates that the age of magical art was fading away. The *t'ao-t'ieh* monster mask, seen on this magnificent *yu*, partakes of the whole animal world. Its form slips elusively through separate features, each of which, alone, might suggest a particular beast, but which, collectively, rage with a truly supernatural ferocity. It is pointless to try and identify the *t'ao-t'ieh* with a specific animal, since only a generalized image could have spoken with a sufficiently universal authority. A generalizing distortion of the particularity of human experience, in the cause of a more universal statement, is a theme that runs right through Chinese art.

Plate 44.
THE PARTING OF SU WU AND LI LING,
attributed to Chou Wen-chü (c. 970);
Southern T'ang dynasty;
handscroll with ink and colours on silk
(detail);
h. 13⅛in., l. 35½in.
National Palace Museum, Taiwan.

Some people do not think of Chinese painting as expressing anything very strongly and even less, would associate it with the expression of strong human emotion, especially as we do not think of the Chinese as a very emotional people. This is very mistaken, however, and there is a tradition of very deep emotion expressed in poetry, which also carried over into painting. The Confucian, though a man of restraint, was expected to feel strongly on many issues. Since Chinese painting in its early centuries, apart from in its service to Buddhism, mainly followed a tradition of Confucian figure subjects, there were many favoured themes of deeply emotional content. This painting is a well-known example. Li Ling and Su Wu were two Chinese generals captured by the Hsiung-nu nomads. Although Li became resigned to his fate and settled into nomad life and Su remained faithful to his emperor, the two endured common adversity. When, after nearly twenty years, the Chinese emperor managed to negotiate Su's release, he returned alone, unable to persuade Li to accompany him. Their final parting was a moment of great agony to them both. This is here portrayed with a violence that would be notable even in Western art. It may owe something to scenes in Buddhist art, such as Mourners at the Physical Death of the Buddha.

Plate 45.
LOHAN,
pottery sculpture with coloured glazes;
Liao dynasty, c. 11th century;
h. 40 9/16 in.
British Museum, London.

Buddhist art is an area in which portraiture had an important role, varying from spiritual portraits of Buddhahood, through imaginary portraits of ancient monastic masters, to portraits from life of contemporary priests. Often involved in these portraits was the transmission of teaching, a factor that naturally encouraged acute psychological perception. This was almost always much more important than the detailed rendering of a face's geography, which was in any case not an ideal concern of China's artistic technology. The life-size figure illustrated here is an imaginary portrait of a Lohan, one of the Buddha's original disciples, and it comes from a magnificent set which is now scattered through the world's museums. The Liao was a Khitan dynasty that ruled across China's northern marches from 907 to 1125. It harboured many conservative traditions of the T'ang and left some fine achievements in ceramics and Buddhist art. The set of Lohans is amongst the greatest Chinese portraiture surviving. We do not know whom the artist used as a model (or models) for this exceptionally intense member of the set, but as a portrait of a man of great wisdom, nourished in the calmness of ascetic discipline, it is hard to match.

Plate 46.
CAMEL AND GROOM,
pottery figurines with green and brown glazes,
from an assembly in the tomb of Liu Ting-hsün (d. 728);
728, T'ang dynasty;
h. of camel 33⅞in., h. of groom 19 3/32 in.
British Museum, London.

The exact reproduction of the physical world was very rarely a primary concern of the Chinese artist and was, indeed, specifically belittled by many critics. Nevertheless, the art of China has depended for its vitality, as much as has the art of any other nation, on acute observation of the physical world and a continuing struggle to translate this into aesthetic form. Interestingly enough, the Chinese often used the most concrete images in talking of the most abstract art—calligraphy. These images, such as a boulder thundering down from a high cliff to smash into the ground, are dynamic. But there are other areas in which observation was translated into forms of immediately striking realism and the most impressive of these is tomb figurines. The custom of populating a tomb with models of the earthly life began well before the Han and achieved its finest expression in the T'ang, when such models were produced in enormous quantity and with great facility. It is remarkable that these productions at once reach so high a standard of artistry and provide so vivid a description of contemporary life. The maker of this camel must have made many others in like mould, but its haughty face and uncooperative attitude are still sharply observed. These Bactrian camels were an essential basis for the busy trade routes stretching through the Central Asian deserts and across to the Middle East.

Plate 47.
ALONG THE RIVER TO THE CAPITAL FOR THE CH'ING-MING FESTIVAL,
by Chang Tse-tuan;
handscroll with ink and colours on silk
(detail);
Northern Sung dynasty, early 12th century;
h. 9¾in., l. 211in.
Chinese Government.

There is in Chinese painting a tradition of narrative depiction with an exactitude of detail that can rival the most documentary of Western art, but it is little known in the West. This painting, by an artist who worked for Emperor Hui-tsung, was executed at the apogee of this tradition. It is a very long horizontal composition, which starts in the countryside and builds up in a crescendo of urban building and bustle until it finally enters the city gate. It must surely count amongst the world's greatest documentaries. The section illustrated shows a climax of a waterway theme, as a frantic crew struggles to guide a great barge sweeping through a narrow bridge, over which streams a mass of humanity which brings with it a new theme, that of the busy streets. We cannot begin to list the multifarious activities, but the ability of the Chinese brush in describing the minute details of everyday life may well be unexpected.

15

Plate 48.

WINTRY FOREST,
by Wen Cheng-ming;
hanging scroll with ink on paper;
dated 1542, Ming dynasty;
h. 35$\frac{7}{16}$in., w. 12$\frac{3}{16}$in.
British Museum, London.

Painting of the *literatus* class served such sophisticated ends, as a profound communication between men in an intimately shared intellectual and artistic tradition, that many of its forms became as conventional as the words of a spoken language. The situation was intensified during the Ming dynasty, when an increasing self-consciousness about the past led many painters to treat their art as a pedantic indulgence of their knowledge about painting of the past. But, even in this period, there are a great many works which appeal to us immediately through their power of description. One subject in which this is especially true is winter trees. Chinese painters were much drawn towards trees, and winter trees in particular had a strong symbolic value. Their bones endured the weather like a man of integrity suffering 'the slings and arrows of outrageous fortune'. Wen Cheng-ming was the most respected of all Ming scholar painters. His obviously acute study of nature is expressed in this very fine work through an exceptional sensitivity in brushwork and subtlety in texture and tone of ink.

HISTORICAL CHART

China			The West
DYNASTIES	DATES	DEVELOPMENTS	EVENTS
Shang	c.1600–1027BC	Bronze Age	c.1350BC Tomb of Pharaoh Tutankhamun
Chou	?1027–221	Rise of feudal states	c.850 Alabaster reliefs from palace of Assyrian King Asurnasirpal III
	5th century	Increasing use of iron	447–432 The Parthenon
	551–479	Confucius	324 End of Alexander the Great's expedition to north-west India
Ch'in	221–206	First unified empire	
Han Former	206BC–AD9	First of great Chinese empires. Beginnings of many institutional and artistic traditions, including the writing brush	
Han Later	25–220	Introduction of Buddhism to China	
	221–589	Six Dynasties period, confused succession of small states, with alien rulers dominating north giving institutional support to Buddhism and vigorous development of cultural traditions under Chinese rulers in the south-east	AD311 Establishment of Christian state by Emperor Constantine
Eastern Chin	317–420	Most famous of states in south, a classic age in poetry, calligraphy and painting	
Northern Wei	386–535	Turkic rulers in the north, patronized Buddhism and construction of massive cave temples	
Northern Ch'i	550–577	One of several small states	
Sui	589–618	Re-unification	
T'ang	618–907	Summit of Chinese wealth and international prestige, basic formation of bureaucratic state. A second classic age of the fine arts. Manufacture of true porcelain	c.650 Sutton Hoo ship burial 687–721 Lindisfarne Gospels 742–814 Emperor Charlemagne
	845	Shattering persecution of Buddhism	
	907–960	Five dynasties period of division. Rapid growth of landscape painting	

China			The West
DYNASTIES	DATES	DEVELOPMENTS	EVENTS
Liao	916–1125	Khitan Tartar rule along northern borders, continuation of some T'ang traditions	
Northern Sung	960–1126	Re-unification. Formulation of aesthetic philosophy by educated elite. Fine arts academies under Emperor Hui-tsung (1101–1125). First identifiable Imperial porcelains	c.1080 The Norman Conquest of England depicted on Bayeux Tapestry 1093–1128 Durham Cathedral
Chin	1115–1234	Jurchid Tartar rulers in north, with continuation of many Northern Sung traditions	
Southern Sung	1127–1279	Tartars control north China; Chinese emperors re-establish capital at Hang-chow in south-east. Well-known painters at southern court academy	?1266–1337 Giotto
Yüan	1279–1368	Mongols encroaching from north finally control all China. Blue and white porcelain. Traditional Chinese bureaucratic class humiliated by Mongol rulers. Intensification of subjective and elitist aesthetic philosophy	
Ming	1368–1644	Last dynasty with Chinese rulers. Diversification and fragmentation of artistic traditions, culminating in limited renascence. Growth of Imperial potteries at Ching-te-chen, with development of enamelled wares	?1390–1441 Jan van Eyck 1452–1519 Leonardo da Vinci 1546–1616 William Shakespeare
Ch'ing	1644–1911	Dynastic house set up by Manchu invaders from north. Rapid sinicization of rulers and flourishing of native artistic traditions under Imperial patronage. Increasingly important patronage by merchant class	1606–1669 Rembrandt 1749–1832 Goethe 1776–1837 John Constable 1839–1906 Paul Cézanne
Republic	1912–1949		
People's Republic	1949–		

1. Bronze libation vessel, *chüeh*, Shang dynasty

3. *Chün* stoneware jar, Chin dynasty

◀ 2. Marble lion, T'ang dynasty

4. Fishing in a Mountain Stream, by Hsü Tao-ning (detail), Northern Sung dynasty

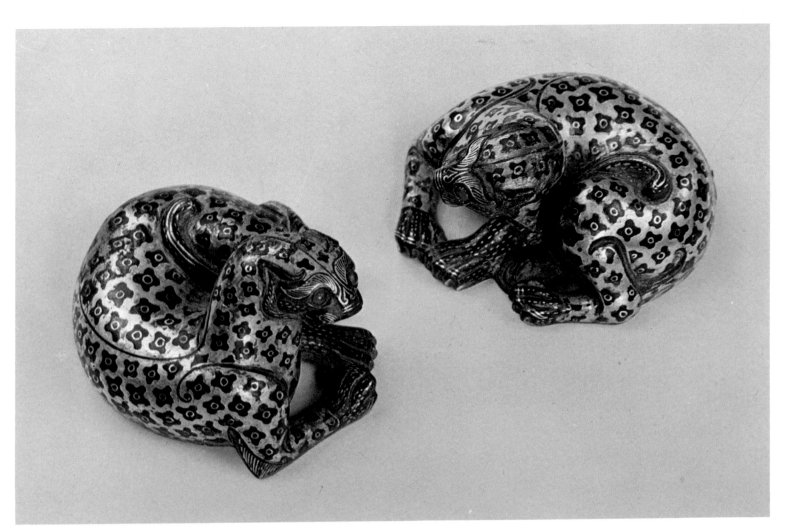

6. Bronze leopards, parcel-gilt with inlay, Western Han dynasty

5, 7. Jade burial suit, Western Han dynasty

千紅萬紫
閱精神
揉得芳菲
色之新
金宮丁氏寫

9. Woodblock colour print, Ming dynasty

◀ 8. Porcelain stem cup, Ch'ing dynasty, Ch'ien-lung era

◀ 10. Bronze ewer, *kuang*, Shang dynasty

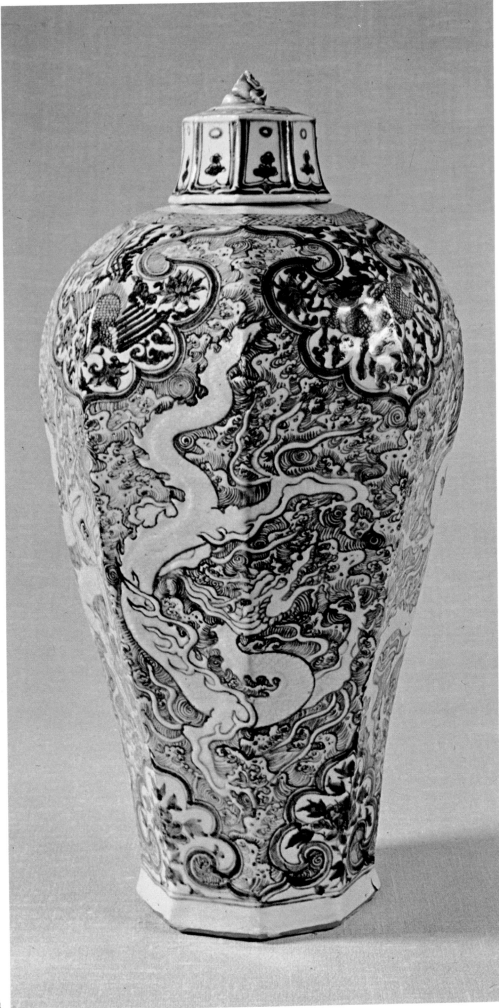

11. Blue and white porcelain jar, Yüan dynasty

12. Carved lacquer boxes, Ming dynasty

13. Bamboo, thorns and birds, by Chang Yen-fu, Yüan dynasty

14. Porcelain stem cup and chicken cup, with over-glaze enamels, Ming dynasty

15. Winter, by Lü Chi (detail), Ming dynasty

迎風呈巧媚

涴露逞紅妍

17. Apricot Blossom, by Ma Yüan, Southern Sung dynasty

◀ 16. Celadon porcelain jar, Sung dynasty

青綠關山迴
嶠崛道路長
宕人多結束行
李自周詳紛
爲名和利那
聲芳與忙年
陳失姓氏北宋
近乎唐
甲午新秋
滄題

18. The Emperor Ming-huang's Flight to Shu (detail), anonymous copy of a T'ang scroll

19. Gold bowl, with repoussé and traced design, T'ang dynasty

21. Tz'u-chou stoneware jar, Sung dynasty

22. Chün stoneware dish, Chin dynasty

25. Pavilion of the Luxuriant Trees, by Shen Shih-ch'ung, Ming dynasty

◀ 24. A Myriad Petals of Jade, by Ch'en Hsien-chang, dated 1437, Ming dynasty

李來蹤跡罕人世
在山鄉半水鄉小閣
臨溪暑退早晴天
雲氣遙衣涼
東廬壽國也　松軒

26, 27. Painting and Calligraphy, by Tao-chi, Ch'ing dynasty

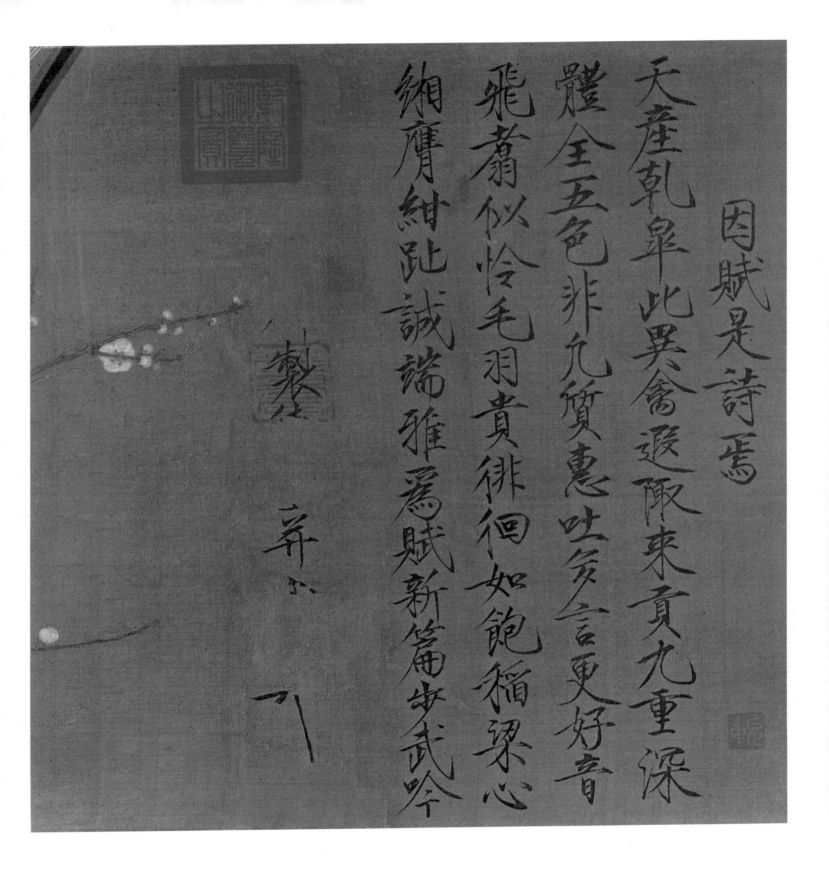

天產乾皐此異禽遐陬來貢九重深

體全五色非凡質惠吐多言更好音

飛肅似憐毛羽貴徘徊如飽稻粱心

緗膺紺趾誠端雅為賦新篇步武吟

因賦是詩焉

製

并書

28, 29. Five-coloured Parakeet, by the Emperor Hui-tsung (details), Northern Sung dynasty

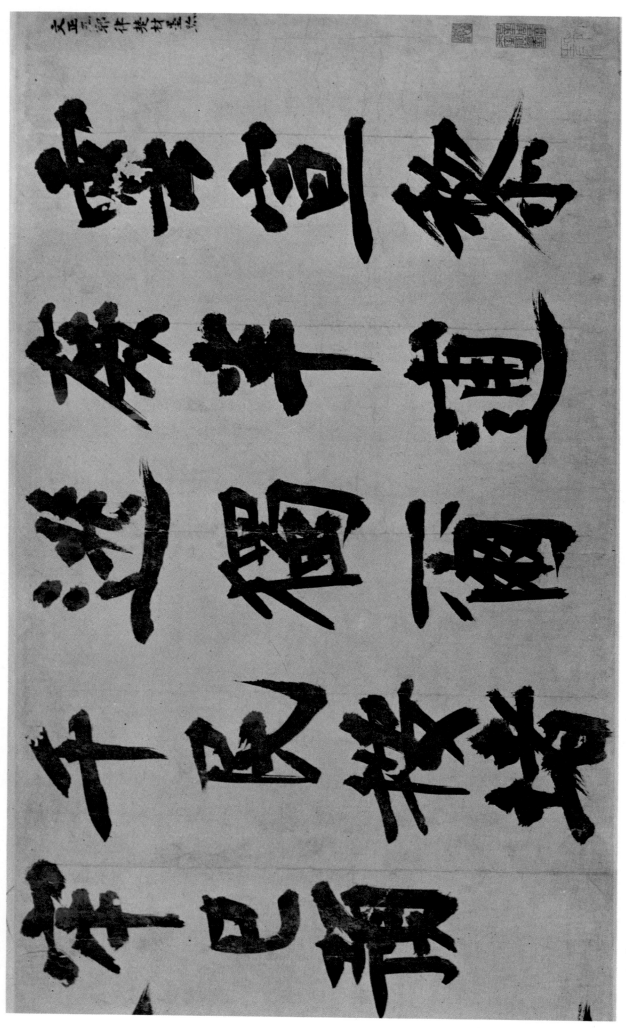

30. Poem of Farewell to a Friend, by Yeh-lü Ch'u-ts'ai (detail), dated 1240, pre-Imperial Yüan dynasty

31. Poems on Flowers, by Chu Yün-ming (detail), dated 1519, Ming dynasty

32. Tartars Travelling on Horseback, by Li Tsan-hua (detail), 10th century, Later T'ang dynasty

33. Vagrants, by Wu Wei (detail), Ming dynasty

34. Bronze horse, Eastern Han dynasty

35. Pottery tomb guardian, T'ang dynasty ▶

防有鵲巢

37. Illustration to the Odes of Ch'en, by Ma Ho-chih (detail), Southern Sung dynasty

◀ 36. Gilt-bronze Buddhist shrine, Northern Wei dynasty

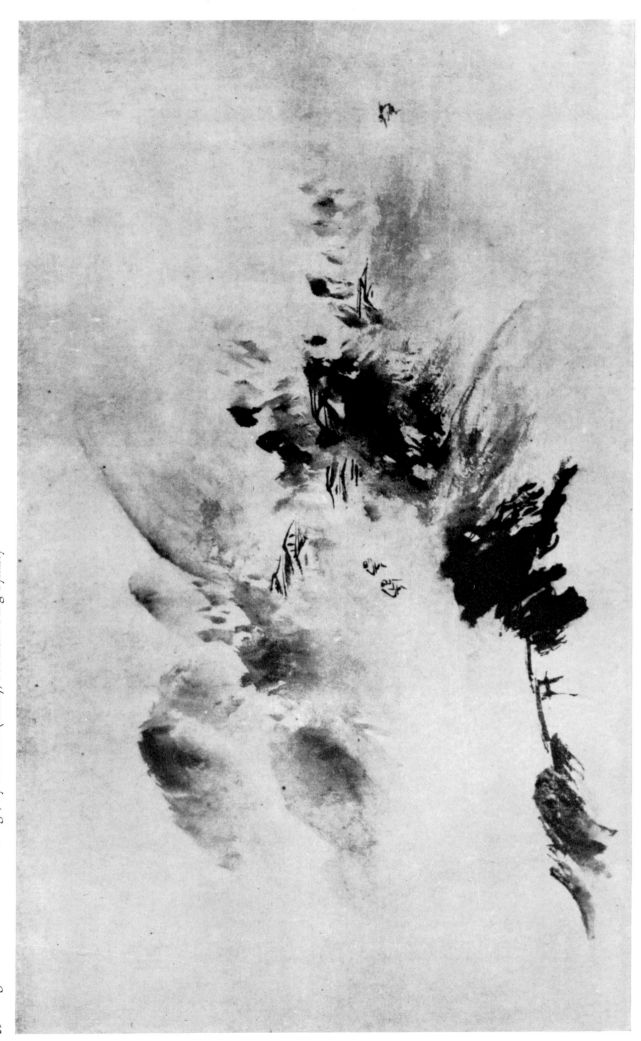

38. The Northern Sea, by Chou Ch'en (detail), Ming dynasty

39. Bright Mists in a Mountain Village, by Yü-chien (detail), Southern Sung dynasty

40. The Coming of Autumn,
by Hung-jen, Ch'ing dynasty

41. Bodhisattva, Northern Ch'i dynasty

42. Immortality under the Great Pine, by Ch'en Hung-shou, dated 1635, Ming dynasty

43. Bronze wine vessel, *yü*, Shang dynasty

44. The Parting of Su Wu and Li Ling, attributed to Chou Wen-chü (detail), Southern T'ang dynasty

45. Lohan, pottery sculpture, Liao dynasty

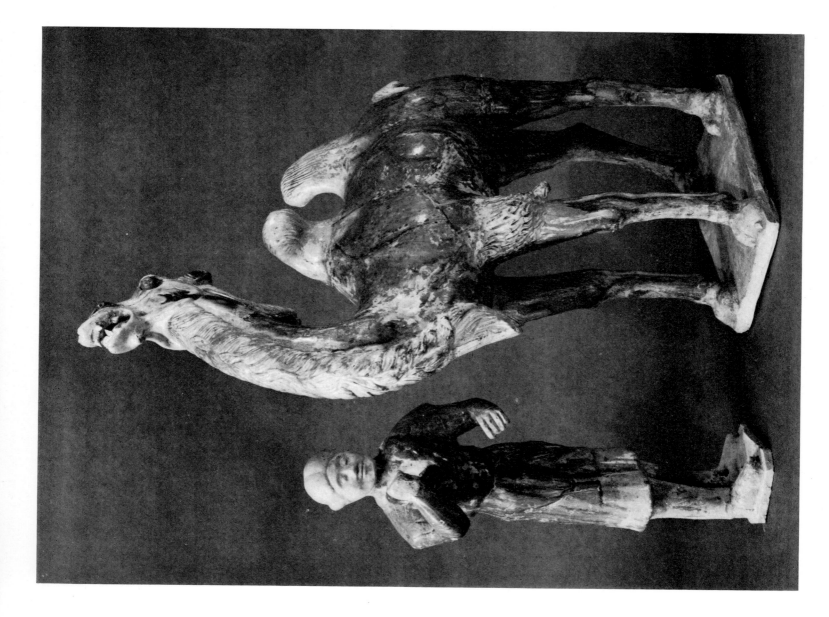